DICKENS

The Dolphin Books

Other titles in preparation

Chatto & Windus

DICKENS

BY

OSBERT SITWELL

London

CHATTO & WINDUS

1932

PRINTED IN GREAT BRITAIN
BY T. AND A. CONSTABLE LTD.
AT THE UNIVERSITY PRESS
EDINBURGH

PR 4588.S4
93665

C

To

HAZEL,

because she loves Dickens
and likes me

DICKENS

Long ago, as I sat engrossed in the adventures of
Oliver Twist, the stupendous towers and flashing
lights of New York, and its clear, frosty night
air, which carries so vibrantly the roar and hoot-
ing of modern traffic, had given way to London ;
a London which consisted of a wide, dark river,
flowing through mile upon mile of crazy, twisted
old houses, set in yellow fog ; a gloomy blossoming
of sudden riches surrounding a golden corolla, ' the
City,' legendary as Dick Whittington to the inhabitants of the remoter suburbs of this undesigned
conglomeration. And then, too, the squares of
Mayfair led an isolated existence, aristocratic and
impersonal, while, as I listened, I seemed almost
to hear the carriages sounding out of a winter's
evening, the horses clapping and stamping the yel-
lowing snow that lay on the roads, with that particular muffled, lolloping rhythm which myself can
recall as a child. . . . Thus reading an English book
in a distant country, not only is its essence dis-

A

tilled for us (as, it is true, is also that of, let us say,
a Russian novel in England) with a peculiar strength
and fragrance, but, even, the features of its author
begin to emerge from the mists of obscurity or the
clouds of legend in which the passing years have
hidden them.

It was time, too, I reflected, in turning over the
pages, that a new and adequate Life of Charles
Dickens was published : for if, as recent biographies
have tended to portray him, he is represented as a
vain, mean, unsympathetic figure, then it must be
plain to all those who know his novels, and can
comprehend them, that this image of him cannot
stand, is utterly false and a travesty. I am not, in
saying this, attempting to concern myself for an
instant with the question of morality in art, being
satisfied, as I look round, that it is by no means
always the nicest people who write the best books,
and, indeed, that many very mean and detestable
persons have written works of transcendent merit,
for, after the fashion of a Mohammedan, I believe
that to a madman it may be given to speak holy
words. Art is outside the individual who voices it :
and how can one cavil at the design of the telephone
that transmits the message ? One can but criticise
its efficiency as an instrument or discuss the relative
perfection with which it accomplishes its task. But,

in this particular case, the matter is an altogether different one : the novels of Dickens are inseparable from the views expounded in them, through the actions of the characters and the consequences that ensue, as much as by the author's personal, and sometimes uncalled for, interference. That he was vain, I am willing to believe : albeit I cannot be persuaded that in his vanity he was without reason ; while, quite apart from this, the creator of 'umble Uriah Heep had cause to despise false humility, and by the very fact of this creation has explained his attitude toward it. But that the warm and gener- ous tones of these books, so pronounced as some- times a little to spoil them, are counterfeit, do not in reality issue from his nature ; that he was not the courageous, affectionate and kindly figure that his writings prove him to be : of these things I can never be convinced. If the facts of his life, as we know them, contradict the impression we have formed at first hand through his work, then it is plain that as we know them—or as we are shown them—these are facts no longer, but lying and misleading statements.

In the novel that was before me the intense charity of his outlook was very discernible. I had reached the passage in *Oliver Twist*—one easy to find because of the Cruikshank drawing that so nobly accompanies it—in which the boy is first introduced into that unforgettable company : ' The walls and ceiling of the room were perfectly black with age and dirt. There was a deal table before the fire : upon which were a candle, stuck in a ginger-beer bottle, two or three pewter pots, a loaf and butter, and a plate. In a frying-pan, which was on the fire, and which was secured to the mantelshelf by a string, some sausages were cooking ; and standing over them, with a toasting-fork in his hand, was a very old shrivelled Jew, whose villainous-looking and repulsive face was obscured by a quantity of matted hair. He was dressed in a greasy flannel gown, with his throat bare ; and seemed to be dividing his attention between the frying-pan and a clothes-horse, over which a great number of silk handkerchiefs were hanging. Several rough beds made of old sacks were huddled, side by side, on the floor. Seated round the table were four or five boys, none older than the " Dodger," smoking long clay pipes, and drinking spirits with the air of middle-aged men. . . .' It was impossible not to read further. . . . ' " We are very glad to see you, Oliver, very," said the Jew. " Dodger, take off the sausages ; and draw a tub near the fire for Oliver. Ah, you're a-staring at the pocket-handkerchiefs ! Eh, my dear ! There are

a good many of 'em, ain't there? We've just looked
'em out, ready for the wash; that's all, Oliver;
that's all. Ha! ha! ha!"...'

A splendid and lively picture, it seemed to me, as
clearly limned as a Dutch interior, every attitude
and accent true: yet how much better, in that it
held to life's action a slightly distorting mirror,
which imparts to the whole composition an added
point and emphasis, the shadows caught by Daumier
or the caustic beauty of a Hogarth or Rowlandson,
where, reversing the usual process, the rind is sweet
and the fruit bitter. How surely, even in his first
words, the Jew reveals his character; the repetition
of Oliver's name, the fawning friendliness of his
address toward him, all underline that oily obse-
quiousness under which lurks a continual menace.
And the words lead you on, induce you to read
just one more sentence and then another. . . .

New York had utterly given way to London—
to the gloomy, slum city of beaver-hatted criminals
—but, as for a moment or two I returned to my
tangible surroundings, it was borne in on me,
more than ever, that a revaluation of Dickens is
due; a further revaluation, for already, during the
last two decades, literary opinion has been forced
to yield him a far higher place than he occupied
formerly. He had, of course, always remained im-

mensely popular with his own very numerous public ; the members of which did not, perhaps, argue the merits of his writing, being content to love it. However, the size and constancy of his audience did, I believe, rather injure than aid him in the consideration of those who are labelled ' discerning.' At any rate, when I was a boy one could not but notice that among those who prided themselves on their love of books, and upon their possession, in this respect, of an educated and cultured taste, it was the fashion to consider Dickens as an author immensely inferior to Thackeray—who in his novels always kept good company, even if he affected to mock at it—and, in fact, to regard him as a somewhat vulgar demagogue and comedian, with a marked gift for appealing to the sentimentality of the crowd. And then, it was said, he was unable to portray ' ladies and gentlemen,' had to be content—for such a deliberate choice was unthinkable—to concern himself with low life, the unpleasant low life of the industrial cities, and never, it was evident, could have dealt, on the one hand, in the subtle psychological reactions of baronets, after the manner of George Meredith, then in his heyday, nor, on the other, have portrayed, with the pen of a Thomas Hardy, the ever-recurring woes of simple-minded but suicidal peasants. The quality of his books, such as it was, they dismissed as an obvious and unfair one : because, even if it were true that, once begun, it was impossible to put down a novel by him (while with Meredith ~~and Hardy~~ it was only too easy), this merely prevented the passing upon him of a calm and cultivated verdict. The very quantity of characters—that grotesque yet deathless army into which he had instilled life—was held to be against him, since this prolificacy proved that the creation of them was easy to him, whereas by then it was well known that ' Genius consists in an infinite capacity for taking pains.'

Already by the time I was grown up, this judgment had been a little reversed. The scale on which he lay was rising, ever so slowly ; while that upon which Meredith had been deposited was sinking—sinking, I may add, far too low. It was at least acknowledged by now that Dickens had been responsible for a whole population of characters, although he was still accused, in his fashioning of them, of ' exaggeration ' ; a charge to which we revert again, albeit the complete refuting of it is the mere fact that every saying and every doing of each person in every book proclaims itself, by its intrinsic rhythm, as pertaining to that particular character and volume.

Now, however much in rebellion against these opinions, it had been difficult, when very young, not to be a little influenced by them : and thus I had been enabled, actually much more surely than if they had been pointed out to me, to appreciate his merits, for I was forced to discover them, little by little, for myself. First of all, it had been necessary to decide which were his best books : and I observed that even those cultured persons who would not admit to a dislike of Dickens invariably singled out two works for their patronising approbation : *A Tale of Two Cities* and *The Pickwick Papers*. With this opinion I very soon found myself in profound disagreement. Indeed, although there are wonderful things in them, I must confess to a very hearty dislike of both these books. One was, to my mind, unbearably sentimental ; while in the other, his humour, generally so founded, as sweetness comes forth from strength, in tragedy and suffering, was too divorced from them for my personal taste. Moreover, it seemed to me that they were not typical, in reality, of his genius : they were apart from the body of his writings : but in precisely that, of course, resided their virtue for those who praised them. . . .

No, as his best books I should now instance *David Copperfield*, *Martin Chuzzlewit*, and *Our*

Mutual Friend. Oliver Twist is certainly not among
them, I thought, turning over the well-known pages
before me, even though it is not the least represen-
tative of its author's excellencies as much as of his
faults, and, in that, may deserve our examination.
It is a long book. The intricacy of its plot is quite
marvellous and allows no flagging of interest. The
action of the hundred pages which precede Chapter
XLIX. is continuous and elaborate, so pleasingly
involved—for it is never fatiguing—that one can
almost observe, as through the glass front of an
old-fashioned clock, the machinery working up for it
to strike. And strike it does! Everyone, in chapter
XLIX., is revealed as some character's brother,
sister or son. The most complex relationships,
worthy of an eighteenth-century Bourbon prince,
are unravelled. Nevertheless, improbable as such
happenings might be outside these pages, within
them they become real, startlingly real. Weighed
down to earth with the living weight of Fagin,
Nancy, the Dodger, and Mr. and Mrs. Bumble, the
book seems solidly anchored to the world we know,
and this illusion is in no way impaired by its fantastic, and yet simple, complication. But, as soon
as the clock has struck, the machinery can be seen
very quickly running down : running down much
faster than it worked up. The concluding chapter

resembles the final scene in a revue or the ultimate ten minutes of a musical comedy. The comedians obtain a last, regretful smile from the wings, even while vice is punished and virtue recompensed. The rewards are as delightful as the punishments are severe—for Dickens, like Saturn, never scruples to devour his children : or, again, after the manner of Abraham, his knife is ever ready to sacrifice when the call sounds. Now the ominous creaking of the halter in the dark wind, which has sounded all through the book, is substantialised. Sikes hangs himself accidentally : Fagin, watching the Judge place the black cap upon his head, listens to the roar of the crowd outside as they hear the news of his sentence : Monks dies of a ' loathesome disease ' : and even the poor Bumbles are doomed to die miserably in the workhouse over which they had so long tyrannised. Everyone else is happily married and sufficiently rich : and we really believe them to be so, such is the actuality of the book ; an extraordinary book. Moreover, as I have said, the very words lead you on, entice you to read chapter after chapter. . . . Surely, notwithstanding there are still those who deny his right to such a description, this is an attribute of the story-teller who is, in addition, an artist ?

At one time myself, too, doubted his title to the

proud word 'artist.' That Dickens was one of the few novelists who, infusing their books with other than purely esthetic notions, had converted them into a weapon, something altogether more charged with seriousness than a mere novel, was, of course, plain from the beginning. Like H.G. Wells after him, he is a prophet: or rather, though not so deliberate and conscious a prophet, his courageous observation verges continually on prophecy. Indeed, his valour is equal to his insight, and the picture, for example, of the United States in *Martin Chuzzlewit* and in his *American Notes* is one that, because of its courteous but devastating veracity, has, even to this day, never been forgiven him in that large continent. Consider this passage, in *American Notes*, and observe how, in its bold diagnosis of the chief evil in the most modern of great nations, it has alas! diagnosed the decay, as it shows itself now, some eighty years after these vehement words were written, of our own older civilisation: for who that to-day looks at the 'stunt' newspapers of England, let alone America, can doubt the truth of them ?

But, the foul growth of America has a more tangled root than this ; and it strikes its fibres deep in its licentious Press. . . . Among the gentry of America ; among the well-informed and moderate : in the learned professions : at the bar and on the bench : there is, as there can be, but one opinion, in reference to the vicious character of these infamous journals. . . . It is sometimes contended—I will not say strangely, for it is natural to seek excuses for such a disgrace—that their influence is not so great as a visitor would suppose. . . .

When any man, of any grade of desert in intellect or character, can climb to any public distinction, no matter what, in America, without first grovelling down upon the earth, and bending the knee before this monster of depravity ; when any private excellence is safe from its attacks ; when any social confidence is left unbroken by it, or any tie of social decency and honour is held in the least regard ; when any man in that free country has freedom of opinion, and presumes to think for himself, and speak for himself, without humble reference to a censorship which, for its rampant ignorance and base dishonesty, he utterly loathes in his heart ; when those who most acutely feel its infamy and the reproach it casts upon the nation, and who most denounce it to each other, dare to set their heels upon, and crush it openly, in the sight of all men : then, I will believe that its influence is lessening, and men are returning to their manly senses. But while that Press has its evil eye in every house, and its black hand in every appointment in the State, from a president to a postman ; while, with ribald slander for its only stock in trade, it is the standard literature of an enormous class, who must find their reading in a newspaper, or they will not read at all ; so long must its odium be upon the country's head, and so long

must the evil it works be plainly visible in the
Republic.

Dickens is not, as we judge from these words, afraid to state the truth. He revels in it, accomplishes it with gusto. Again, like Mr. H. G. Wells after him, he was, as a writer, an exponent, among other things, of direct action, and was able visibly to change during his lifetime, by force of the ideas so ably advocated through the medium of his fiction, the everyday existence round him. However, this propaganda was not political, philosophic or scientific, as it is with the later novelist, but consisted of an invocation, in no way sentimental in itself despite the indisputable sentimentality of various passages, to humanitarian feeling; of a plea to ameliorate conditions in a world which, owing to the growth of the great cities, had become visibly harder, more muddled and more brutal. And, through the agency of his works, the lives of thousands of human beings, in hospitals and workhouses, factories, slums and prisons, had, indeed, been improved out of all recognition. All this was clear, established beyond argument. Nevertheless, at first one wondered whether the cultured and plausible criticism which has been cited could be wholly erroneous and obtuse, and, since there was obviously more to his novels than it allowed, inclined to accept him as a production altogether English ; a great *maker of novels*, a great novelist who stood outside the boundaries of art, just in the same manner that in these days it is possible, through a reliance on engineering instead of architecture, to be a great builder without deserving to be called a great architect.

Yet, being a reader who prefers books of the opposite category, that have too much, rather than too little, art in them—for I care in my very bones for the shape of a book and the colour and texture of it, delight in imagery and the kindred arts of stimulating, if only for the release they give to the mind, and cannot help but feel violently opposed to those blunt, straightforward chronicles of life, in the office and out of it, couched in ' business man's prose,' which in England deck themselves out as ' fiction '—a want of this quality quickly communicates itself to me. But no such lack was to be detected in these novels : they satisfied the imagination. It was, in fact, impossible for long to mistake their appeal ; one which was, undoubtedly, based on art, however much their author was unaware himself of the nature of it, or why he wrote in this way, and however much, again, he disguised and even sunk it. Thus gradually the conviction established itself that he was

an artist, and not the indigenous and isolated
English phenomenon I have described.

And here, then, as I had sat reading *Oliver Twist*,
I became convinced that fresh claims should be en-
tered for him in respect of two particulars: as the
originator of the modern 'thriller,' the father—and
a parent how much more lively and entertaining
than his children!—to Sherlock Holmes and all
the numerous subsequent tales of crime detected
through coincidence or by means of consummate
ability and then punished with a striking and
enviably appropriate justice; and, far more important, as an artist who, quite apart from being a
born story-teller, with, in addition, an indescribable
gift of words, had contrived to equip himself with
an extraordinary and personal technique.

The first claim, that he is a master of sensational
plots and continued excitement, that it is difficult
to stop reading a book by him, so powerfully does
the action of it grip you, is the more easily sub-
stantiated and can, indeed, hardly be contested.
The second is more difficult to establish, for many,
even of those who love him, are so blinded by the
splendour of his humanitarian achievement, or have
so sated themselves with the variety and richness
of his humour, that it seems to them of minor
importance : while those who dislike his writings

will reject it outright. Once, however, that these two claims are admitted, the problem becomes all the more pressing of a just and proper critical estimate of his work, and its examination more fascinating.

One must begin, nevertheless, with an admission. It has to be confessed that Dickens was ignorant, and innocent, of art outside himself, and was, moreover, unresponsive to it. Indeed, not aware in this of his own hypocrisy—the vice he most despised—and sharing the genuine anti-art bias which has possessed most English people since the triumph of Cromwell and the Puritans, he was apt in his novels to ridicule the artist. It will be noticed throughout his works that any figure approximating to this category—Mr. Skimpole, for example —is made to look ludicrous, and this attitude undoubtedly, I think, helped him with his large public, who, thus feeling secure, read his books without any suspicion that these, too, were the work of an artist, and no inconsiderable one. But his own art was emotional and instinctive. In other things than matters of criticism, poetry and painting, he exhibited a very poor taste : (though in this last respect it deserves to be noted that, through some stroke of good fortune, he is nearly the only English novelist to find an illustrator worthy of him, for Cruikshank is a great interpreter). His *Travels in*

Italy show him to be without much feeling for the marvels of architecture or the incidental and romantic beauty of that epoch in the peninsula.

But when all this (and it is quite enough to have to say of such an artist) has been said, one can but marvel at the immensity of his achievement in spite of it.

Certainly Charles Dickens was the earliest English novelist to comprehend the haphazard and ramshackle romance of the great nineteenth-century cities, the first to be able to dramatise and present it to the world ; in this the fore-runner of countless writers. Indeed, he depicts these strange and terrible conglomerations, the life that slinks through their alleys as much as the sudden ebullitions of the market-places, with an unequalled mastery and insight. The teeming existence, a riot or a mob running after a pick-pocket, is not reproduced more faithfully, or more formidably, than the sinister vacuums which its turmoil shelters. Consider the ' Stop-thief ! ' passage in which the mistaken crowd pursues Oliver Twist : and think then of the opening of *Our Mutual Friend*, and the boat upon the black waters of the Pool of London. In example of the lifeless and secret spots, let us bring to mind the beginning of *Bleak House*, where the thick brown fog

B

preserves, in a sort of half-life, the solicitor's office from which we obtain our first perspective of a complicated drama, just as the thick brown varnish preserves the marbled paper on its walls. Or, again, there is the following page from *Oliver Twist*, which combines both qualities of description :

> Near to that part of the Thames on which the church at Rotherhithe abuts, where the buildings on the banks are dirtiest and the vessels on the river blackest with the dust of colliers and the smoke of close-built low-roofed houses, there exists the filthiest, the strangest, the most extraordinary of the many localities that are hidden in London, wholly unknown, even by name, to the great mass of its inhabitants.
>
> To reach this place, the visitor has to penetrate through a maze of close, narrow and muddy streets, thronged by the roughest and poorest of waterside people, and devoted to the traffic they may be supposed to occasion. The cheapest and least delicate provisions are heaped in the shops ; the coarsest and commonest of wearing apparel dangle at the salesman's door, and stream from the house parapet and windows. Jostling with unemployed labourers of the lowest class, ballast-heavers, coal-whippers, brazen women, ragged children, and the raff and refuse of the river, he makes his way with difficulty along, assailed by offensive sights and smells from the narrow alleys which branch off on the right and left, and deafened by the clash of ponderous waggons that bear great piles of merchandise from the

stacks of warehouses that rise from every corner. Arriving, at length, in streets remoter and less-frequented than those through which he has passed, he walks beneath tottering house-fronts, projecting over the pavement, dismantled walls that seem to totter as he passes, chimneys half crushed, half hesitating to fall, windows guarded by rusty iron bars that time and dirt have almost eaten away, every imaginable sign of desolation and neglect.

In such a neighbourhood, beyond Dockhead in the Borough of Southwark, stands Jacob's Island, surrounded by a muddy ditch, six or eight feet deep and fifteen or twenty wide when the tide is in, once called Mill Pond, but known in the days of this story as Folly Ditch. It is a creek or inlet from the Thames, and can always be filled at high water by opening the sluices at the Lead Mills from which it took its old name. At such times, a stranger, looking from one of the wooden bridges thrown across it at Mill Lane, will see the inhabitants of the houses on either side lowering from their back doors and windows, buckets and pails, domestic utensils of every kind, in which to haul the water up; and when his eye is turned from these operations to the houses themselves, his utmost astonishment will be excited by the scene before him. Crazy wooden galleries common to the backs of half-a-dozen houses, with holes from which to look upon the slime beneath; windows, broken and patched, with poles thrust out on which to dry the linen that is never there; rooms so small, so filthy, so confined, that the air would seem too tainted even for the dirt and squalor which they shelter; wooden chambers thrusting themselves out above the mud, and threatening to fall into it—as some have done ; dirt-besmeared walls and decaying foundations ; every repulsive lineament of poverty, every loathe-some indication of filth, rot and garbage ; all these ornament the banks of Folly Ditch.

So true are his descriptions, not, it must be allowed, to the modern, cosmopolis-skyscraper conception of a German or American city, but to the dreary and tortuous wastes that still exist everywhere in England, forming a very real, if not particularly pleasant, side of our civilisation, and one that seems, withal, as if it may, with its subse-quent entangling apparatus of road, railway and bungalow, wholly destroy in the end our older and more traditional life, that we are constantly sur-prised to discover how long ago they were written. (*Oliver Twist*, for example, was published first in 1838.) And, recalled for an instant to my sur-roundings, I wondered how this author was at present appreciated—apart from those people who will ever dislike him for his truthful remarks about America—in this large continent, where cities have developed for themselves a new perspective, a vista that is vertical instead of horizontal. For whereas New York and Chicago are ' climbers,' London must ever remain a ' crawler ' of a town, thereto bound by its very nature. In that resides

its romance, as we see from the foregoing passage.
. . . But in New York and such logically developed
centres no stranger can lose his way on the ground:
although once in the air, it is almost impossible for
him to find it, so high are these cliffs, so full of floors,
and he must hurry in and out of lifts that climb
more quickly than the fabulous beanstalk which
enabled Jack to deal with the Giant. No criminal
can slink through a warren or up an alley : he is
no Fagin or Sikes, but wears ' immaculate evening dress ' and a mask, and stands at bay on a
brilliantly illuminated staircase.   Nevertheless,
though this type of evil is beyond Dickens' scope,
he would, no doubt, have revelled, however shocked
by it, in the secretive side of American life ; the
speak-easies and racketeering. That he could draw
American characters, we know from the pages of
Martin Chuzzlewit.

But what is the use of such surmises ? Dickens
is, and ever will be, London. His writings reflect
it at every angle, and even if at times his accounts
of the underworld verge on melodrama, are sometimes a little strained, yet they never fail of effect.
And what a relief, in these days of ' under-writing '
as of ' under-acting,' to read full-bodied prose with
plenty of contours. . . . We are never left in un-
certainty of the direction in which the language is

hitting. It contains nothing empty and undirected. But the most patent sign of his genius is that, after having read the whole passage, we find that its effect is far greater than we could have imagined from the perusal of any individual sentence in it, or than, indeed, we can explain.

But however clearly such extracts as we have quoted show him to be a master novelist and an artist in writing, his delineation of character proves it to a still greater degree, and places him above ordinary criticism, in a class by himself with no contemporary rival. Here we see him, again, as a prototype, an innovator, wielding with perfect ease a technique toward which others are even now but struggling; the inventor of ' expressionism ' in fiction—a writer a hundred years ahead of his time. All the properties of his characters are perfectly fitted to them, and have been designed to reveal their disposition and heighten the appropriateness of it to their appearance, and, beyond that, to facilitate their various courses through the book. For these purposes, too, he makes use of a wilful and superb distortion, perfectly maintained and congruous throughout each novel, and one which bestows upon its objects ever so much more of an authentic existence than could any merely ' life-like ' method. Imagery now comes to his aid,

to endow him with an unimaginable virtuosity.
Page after page could be quoted in support of these
statements, and, indeed, it is difficult to refrain
from giving them . . . that tremendous supper-
party, staged by the Kenwigs in honour of the
Collector of Water Rates, from *Nicholas Nickleby*;
the dinner given by the Veneerings in *Our Mutual
Friend*: but we must be content with one or two
short quotations from *David Copperfield*, which,
however, should suffice. The first is a description
of the warder-like Miss Murdstone, sister to David's
stepfather, on his first seeing her:

> It was Miss Murdstone who was arrived, and a
> gloomy-looking lady she was; dark, like her brother,
> whom she greatly resembled in face and voice; and
> with very heavy eyebrows, nearly meeting over her
> large nose, as if, being disabled by the wrongs of
> her sex from wearing whiskers, she had carried them
> to that account. She brought with her two uncom-
> promising black boxes, with her initials on the lids
> in hard brass nails. When she paid the coachman she
> took her money out of a hard steel purse, and she kept
> the purse in a very jail of a bag which hung from
> her arm by a heavy chain, and shut up like a bite.

And, again of the same lady:

> She began to 'help' my mother next morning,
> and was in and out of the store closet all day,
> putting things to rights, and making havoc in the
> old arrangements. Almost the first remarkable

thing I observed in Miss Murdstone was her being constantly haunted by a suspicion that the servants had a man secreted somewhere on the premises. Under the influence of this delusion, she dived into the coal-cellar at the most untimely hours, and scarcely ever opened the door of a dark cupboard without clapping it to again, in the belief that she had got him.

Though there was nothing very airy about Miss Murdstone, she was a perfect Lark in point of getting up. She was up (and, as I believe to this hour, looking for that man) before anybody in the house was stirring.

No commercial writer, no pure student of life, no simple philanthropist, no one but a consummate artist ever slanted his pen at such an angle : yet such instances of swift and masterful distortion are exactly what those who attempt to dismiss this great writer mean, when they charge him with ' exaggeration ' !

Nevertheless, having to our own satisfaction established him on this highest level, as a very great novelist who invented for himself his own supreme technique, we are left with the curious problem of an art wherein the faults are as salient and consistent as the merits. How, we ask ourselves, as we find sentence after sentence that would, in other writers, place them beyond our endurance, forcing us to abandon wholly and for

ever the effort to read their books, how (and why)
does he do it ? How *could* he write such stuff ?
And then, even while we are yet querulous, we
realise that we have finished the chapter and are
beginning the next ; which will in all probability
compensate us in full for our suffering. Thus, in
Oliver Twist, having disgusted his discerning readers
with the appallingly fatuous and maudlin first
interview between Rose Maylie and Nancy, Dickens
proceeds at once to give them pages of unsurpassed
brilliance and interest. Chapter follows chapter,
each better than the last ; the second interview, on
the steps of London Bridge, is good ; the slaughter
of Nancy by Sikes, wonderful ; and, finally, the
author rises on the wings of his genius to that
terrific scene where Charley Bates throws himself
upon Nancy's murderer. Herein Dickens achieves
one of the most difficult feats known to the writer
of fiction, insomuch as he causes a character,
created and all through the book produced as
essentially comic, to be transmuted to the heights
of heroism without a seeming flaw or any break in
its apparent continuity.

Even so, the question remains to be answered :
how has he persuaded us to read on ? For our per-
sistence is not owing solely and altogether to the
knowledge that his lapses will be atoned for by the

delights to follow them. No, the answer, I think, is rather that he carries us through these perilous straits by the rush and energy of his prose; ' energy ' I use for want of a better word, seeking to indicate a singular fusing of fluency and a continual sense of direction with the power to depict in words that will automatically arouse in the reader the emotion intended. There are those, I know, who object bitterly to the prose-style of the author, or altogether deny him one, charging him with a tendency to dip into unintentional blank verse [1] whenever he wishes to move us . . . yet any prose-style that sweeps the reader on with it is justified. How often, in the work of a stylist, does one not discover that it is the very style, for which the author is so renowned, that holds the reader in check, acting as a barrier between transmitter and receiver? Moreover, about Dickens' use

[1] He is not the only author guilty of this eccentricity. I remember a well-known novelist, a contemporary of mine, who was, some fifteen years ago, a dramatic critic. On one occasion he was representing his paper at the first night of a play by a celebrated old playwright. He found the blank verse of it monotonous, and said so in print the next morning, complaining that its example proved how impossible it was to write a modern play in metre. In answer the playwright wrote a letter, couched in very injured terms to the Editor of the journal, pointing out that his play was not written in verse at all, but in prose.

of language, even when he is being sentimental, there is nothing namby-pamby. And if only some of the more precious authors, who object to his manner, would display, among their arrangement of words which recall those Victorian screens that were composed of designs carried out in decaying autumn leaves and then pressed flat under glass, one tittle of his inspired vigour, we would willingly forgive them whole folios of fortuitous blank verse.

Furthermore, it is possible that in addition to this quality of energy there is another reason for the success with which he leads on, so triumphantly, to the end of each book. As a thing apart and by itself, the design of his novels, I hold, is of a finer order than many people allow : and who knows but that the sickly passages alluded to, help to observe throughout the book an abstract function of integral balance which is of actual esthetic service to it ? And then the vulgarity, such as it is, of these portions is so evident, frank and childlike, so small a thing compared with that fire of generosity, which is its counterpart and flickers under every page, that we are disarmed. For the appeal to sentimentality is direct, even clumsily direct and melodramatic ; never morbidly insinuating or wistfully graceful, as are those passages in which Sir James Barrie, for example, stifles his understanding sobs. And which man of taste is there who would not prefer the most ostentatiously dying, the most indelicately delicate, of Dickens' doomed children to that sexless, but elfin whimsey, Peter Pan ?

But we have not, of course, set ourselves the task of classing him with such an exponent of pathos, any more than, on the other hand, with such a stylist as Sterne. How, rather, can these novels be matched against, not, let us say, the intellectually distinguished work of Meredith, but against books more vital ? . . . Let us compare them with those of Dostoieffsky, whom so many people consider the greatest novelist of all time. . . . Is it possible that there is a parallel to be traced between these two writers ? At first it may seem absurd, because Russian and Englishman is each so intensely national in his flavour. Yet both are artists : and both, despite that honour, seek in the first place to serve humanity ; a purpose of which, occasionally, supreme novels are made the vehicle, though, as may be deduced from the great and exquisite work of Flaubert, it is not intrinsically necessary to them. Both writers, again, are adept at the description of horror, can communicate a haunting sense of fear, an atmosphere of gathering violence and evil, which, developed to this degree, is an unusual ability : and it is not easy, for instance, to decide whether the murder of Mr. Montague Tigg or that in *Crime and Punishment* is the more awe-inspiring and convincing. Each author, too, introduces pages that are irritating in the extreme, so that the reader cries ' If only some one would edit them ! ' and then, omitting to read them, feels their loss, since it is equally impossible to condense *The Brothers Karamazoff* or *Martin Chuzzlewit*. Dostoieffsky does not, it is true, apostrophise to the same enraging extent as Dickens : but then, again, Dickens is guiltless of the soft, pulpy mysticism, that reverse side of the ' knout-spirit,' in which Dostoieffsky revels, and spares us, too, the masses of private but muddled thinking in which the characters of the Russian novelist indulge. On the other hand, both these authors betray alike in every line they pen a strong moral sense ; albeit in Dostoieffsky's case one that is so completely perverted that, had he composed *Oliver Twist*, Fagin and Sikes would have constituted, rather than the villains, the epileptic and murderous but still interesting and immensely psychological heroes of the story. Indeed, toward the end of it, Dickens himself appears inclined to adopt what may perhaps be termed a Russian view of Fagin : and the horrible old Jew, as he sits, with a bandage round his head, biting his nails in the condemned cell, is transformed into a somewhat more pitiable and less repellent character. But this is unusual with the Englishman. His villains are to be considered as villains, and he obviously enjoys paying them back in their own coin ; a necessity which Dostoieffsky always, as plainly, regrets. In fact, notwithstanding that both novelists make a continual plea for the under-dog, thoroughly to earn Dostoieffsky's sympathy the under-dog must be rabid into the bargain.

' But,' it may be urged, ' even if you insist on comparing these two writers, how do you reconcile your love for Dickens with your admiration for Flaubert, and the French novel ? ' And here, passing on to discuss this point, we may pause to note something at first a little strange, even disconcerting : for, seemingly remote as is the work of Charles Dickens from that of any French novelist, yet it is possible that he has exercised an influence in a very unexpected quarter. Thus, a correspondent [1] in the columns of the *Times Literary Supplement* has recently drawn attention to

---

[1] *Times Literary Supplement*, February 19th, 1931 : ' Sir, I wonder whether those who have already been struck by the resemblance which Marcel Proust bears to Charles Dickens—whom, it is well known, he read with that luminous enthusiasm and comprehension characterising him—have remembered a certain passage in *Dombey and Son* which I venture to submit as one of the most extra-

a similarity between a passage in *Dombey and Son* and the style subsequently affected by Marcel Proust; the outlook and sentiments expressed are, of course, very different, yet the resemblance is so distinct that, if purely coincidence, then it ranks as prophecy on the part of the older writer. It is more probable, though, that Proust, who, as we

ordinary instances of an anticipated form of thought and style in literature?

' " He did not know why. For all that the child observed, and felt, and thought, that night—the present and the absent; what was then and what had been—were blended like the colours in the rainbow, or in the plumage of rich birds when the sun is shining on them, or in the softening sky when the same sun is setting. The many things he had had to think of lately, passed before him in the music; not as claiming his attention over again, or as likely ever more to occupy it, but as peacefully disposed of and gone. A solitary window, gazed through years ago, looked out upon an ocean, miles and miles away; upon its waters, fancies, busy with him only yesterday, were hushed and lulled to rest like broken waves. The same mysterious murmur he had wondered at, when lying on his couch upon the beach, he thought he still heard sounding through his sister's song, and through the hum of voices, and the tread of feet, and having some part in the faces flitting by, and even in the heavy gentleness of Mr. Toots, who frequently came up to shake him by the hand. Through the universal kindness he still thought he heard it, speaking to him; and even his old-fashioned reputation seemed to be allied to it, he knew not how."

' Truly yours,

' M. CIOLKOWSKA.

' Via Del Babiuno 46. Rome.'

know, greatly esteemed various English authors of the Age of Steam—George Eliot and Ruskin, for instance—was thoroughly acquainted with the works of Dickens, and, more sensitive than most of his contemporaries, appreciated it at its true worth.

Indeed, we can see that there would be much in it that would captivate him in this singularly alien yet familiar world : for just as Dickens, where his sense of Victorian decency was not outraged, would surely have found Madame Verdurin congenial company, so Proust must immensely have enjoyed such expositions of Dickens' social sense as the supper, already referred to, in *Nicholas Nickleby*, given in honour of the Collector of Water Rates, or the Veneering dinner. (One cannot help but wonder, however, what Dickens would have thought of the Baron de Charlus, and how, had this gentleman insisted on coming to life in his mind, he would have treated this same character ?) But the likeness is one of imagination and phrasing, as well as of humour. The passage from *Dombey and Son* exists entirely on the imaginative plane. And let us now, in pursuit of this queer comparison, read out of the book before us a few sentences from that chapter in which Mr. Brownlow, meeting Oliver Twist for the first time, is searching his memory for the person of whom the child reminds him.

After musing for some minutes, the old gentleman walked, with the same meditative face, into a back anteroom opening from the yard; and there, retiring into a corner, called up before his mind's eye a vast amphitheatre of faces, over which a dusky curtain had hung for many years. . . . He wandered over them again. He had called them into view, and it was not easy to replace the shroud that had so long concealed them. There were the faces of friends, and foes, and of many that had been almost strangers peering intrusively from the crowd: there were faces of young and blooming girls that were now old women; there were faces that the grave had changed and closed upon, but which the mind, superior to its power, still dressed in their old freshness and beauty, calling back the lustre of the eyes, the brightness of the smile, the beaming of the soul through its mask of clay, and whispering of beauty beyond the tomb, changed but to be heightened, and taken from the earth only to be set up as a light, to shed a soft and gentle glow upon the path to Heaven.

Can one not detect in this passage, although it lacks the scientific level-headed tone of Proust, something a little Proustian in phrasing and conception?

It must be admitted, however, that Proust is his own tradition, and, save in the ingenious working of his mind and its responsiveness, is not so peculiarly French as are Flaubert and Maupassant. Is it, then, within reason to proclaim as great authors, and in the same breath, Dickens and his complete antithesis Flaubert : the Englishman, often so diffuse, his art a child of nature, untutored and rather unlettered even, his stories so intricate and full of knots, turn and double-turn, so free from artistic theories, albeit so crammed with humanitarian propaganda, his characters so prisoned in their own world ; the Frenchman, clear and compact in his thinking, so educated, his novels so carefully observed and studied, though still containing all the fire that was ever breathed into an author's work to be expressed with the perfection of skill and the utmost poetic feeling ? Flaubert's intellect was doubtless of a higher, less fantastic order : in his work there is nothing unbalanced, everything has been passed through the exquisitely fine sieve of his understanding and sensitiveness. There is no direct appeal to the emotions, and his books are esthetic entities, not tinged in the least with propaganda of any kind. But even his infinitely more subtle and lovely creations do not, if they are focussed from the distance, stand out clearer or live longer in the memory than do the so recognisable and individual ones of Dickens. And ' memorability ' is a quality that pertains, in this sense, to the novel, much as the memorability of certain lines is often a test of verse.

Thus in the full sense of their greatness, utterly contrasting in detail, I apprehend they are comparable. Never perhaps can we hope to bring forth a novelist of such imaginative perfection, so polished, and at the same time so full of fire, as Flaubert: but we may, notwithstanding, give birth to one who, after the manner of the Russian authors, will be in a sense more important. It is impossible to exaggerate the significance for us of Dickens: and the clue to the difference that exists between him and any Continental novelist must be sought in the simple fact of his nationality. The English, even though for a decade or two at a time they may affect European manners and modes of thought, are individual to the same almost absurd extent as the Russians, Spanish or Japanese. However manifold and widely spread are our possessions, we cannot, try as we will, behave or think in a Continental fashion. And Dickens is a production altogether and peculiarly English, as English as Shakespeare or Pope. All the racial characteristics are to be traced in his work: and this, added to the excitement of his plots, is the explanation of the hold he has always maintained upon a large public, not usually given to reading: a public which can, even to-day, recognise that his types are true ones, living all round them, and to whom the ways of thinking indulged in by any foreign writer would seem alien and even eccentric.

Moreover, after the fashion of so many artists of our land, his creative impulse is deep rooted in, or, as some may think, inextricably entangled with, motives of morality. Often, when it is a visual picture he conjures up for us—and, indeed, he is a very pictorial writer—we are reminded of Hogarth. The scenes in Newgate, by painter and writer, even though the passing of a century divides one from the other, are practically identical, interchangeable : (and how exact an interpretation of the time and place they were can be inferred from the corroborative and pathetic pages of W. B. Haydon's Autobiography). ' Marriage à la Mode ' or ' The Rake's Progress ' is the equivalent of Dickens' writing. There is to be distinguished in them, in picture and in book, the same ethic foundation, the same love and use of detail in illustration of the theme, the same democratic distrust of a ' profligate aristocracy '[1] : a suspicion engendered in part by

[1] This is very obvious in all Hogarth's moral scenes. Compare with them the conversation between Mrs. Kenwigs, Mr. Lillyvick, and Miss Petowker, ' of the Theatre Royal, Drury Lane,' concerning the personal appearance of Nicholas Nickleby.

' He has a very nice face and style, really,' said Mrs. Kenwigs. ' He certainly has,' added Miss Petowker.

the more cosmopolitan tendency of the richer
classes. Further, that vein of savagery, that love
of the grotesque, which runs through so much of
the best English literary and pictorial work of the
eighteenth and early nineteenth centuries, is very
manifest in both of them : although in these two
instances harnessed to a purely humanitarian purpose, which bestows upon it a double force. Nevertheless, just as our caricaturists and cartoonists,
when they were effective and propagandist (instead
of being content, as now they are, to hold up a
flattering mirror to the countenance of the middle
classes), appeared to delight in deformities such as
acromegaly, elephantiasis, and facial distortion ; to
find material for ferine and raucous laughter in
bloated faces, red and warty, in protruding teeth,
long, nut-cracker chins, purple, fungoid noses, in
figures gigantically, horribly fat, or so wasted as to
show the flat and angular bones, and a thousand

'There is something in his appearance quite—dear, dear,
what's that word again ? '

' What word ? ' inquired Mr. Lillyvick.

' Why—dear me, how stupid I am,' replied Miss
Petowker. ' What do you call it, when Lords break off
door-knockers and beat policemen, and play at coaches
with other people's money, and all that sort of thing ? '

' Aristocratic ? ' suggested the collector.

' Ah ! aristocratic,' replied Miss Petowker ; ' something
very aristocratic about him, isn't there ? '

other forms of physical anomaly; so, too, Dickens makes use of a certain brutal emphasis, though this has been somewhat levigated by the growing politeness of the nineteenth century, and is never employed except in order to engage the pity of the reader or arouse his anger on behalf of 'true justice.' But if such an aim was, in his eyes, necessary to excuse the means, it must be owned that the virtuosity of his method betrays a certain satisfaction in it : for there was nothing amorphous about his Christian kindness, and it was inspired by a sharply outlined and crusading spirit. After this manner, too, his illustrator, Cruikshank (himself a reformed drunkard and an artist who perceived the grotesque aspects of intoxication), underlines and exaggerates, draws every possible fantastic quality out of the caprices which a love of too much liquor imposes upon its devotees, but always with the design of moral improvement, always as a caution and warning. And yet we feel, to depict them so well, must not himself have enjoyed a little witnessing these distressing scenes and symptoms ? Thus Dickens appears often to delight in describing the repulsive manners and ill-favoured countenances of his villains ; at which, indeed, he is often more convincing than when he sings the charms of his simple and blushing heroines. But,

though he could dwell in this fashion on the
physical aspect of his characters, English morality
now enters in, to prevent any discussion of physical
relationships : and the love of the hero for the
heroine is a thing altogether Victorian, divorced
absolutely from the animal world whence man
is descended. He will describe a woman dying in
childbirth and out of wedlock, with charity, sympathy and understanding : but we feel that the
child might as well have been found in a rose-bush
or between the leaves of a cabbage, and that its
birth was due to no physical union. Nevertheless
this attitude, since it attains the force of a literary
convention, does not destroy the power of his
works.

Further, not only has Dickens this moralistic
basis and bias that we have noted—so alien to the
spirit of any French author—but he displays in the
working out of his books that extraordinary English
team-spirit, cultivated in all branches of our life,
however unfortunate, from politics to athletics,
from athletics to the editing of *Punch* : so that
throughout his every novel we witness what can
only be described as a ‘Virtue *v.* Vice Cup-Tie
Final.’ But, though we are aware from the beginning, as the result of experience, that the poor
and good will triumph after a hotly-disputed match,

this constant intuition is never allowed to spoil the reality of his books or cramp their appeal to the reader : on the contrary, he is artist enough to capture our interest and retain it until the finish.

Even in Dickens' minor traits, one cannot but be surprised how his intensely national flavour emerges. Thus, whatever our faults, I take it that we are a generous nation, giving freely of our money—too freely—and somewhat disposed to hold thrift, whether national or particular, in contempt. Moreover, we like the individual who spends easily, taking not too much heed for the morrow. And, similarly, when we read Dickens, we observe that his heroes are never concerned for their next day's bread. Prudence and forethought, it is evident, are not the virtues upon which he set store. Quite penniless and without prospect, his favourites never hesitate to knock down their stingy employer and flounce out of the office, and, as Elijah was fed, so their creator delights to provide for them. Avarice is for him the cardinal sin. Indeed, the greatest obloquy, the deepest circle of his hell, is reserved for the miser, who in the literature of other and more economically-minded nations, such as the French or Dutch, might be extolled as hero ; a dear, careful old man, engaged in self-denial in order to bequeath a fortune to his heirs. But no

wickedness which Mr. Ralph Nickleby accomplishes
is, we are made to feel, blacker than his money-
lending and money-saving : while, again, in reading
Oliver Twist, we begin to perceive that the real
offence of Fagin, far worse than any crimes he
committed or caused to be committed, was that of
hoarding up his tainted treasure. Let us consider
this little picture of one who in the novels of
other nations might be raised to the status of an
' international financier and philanthropist ' :

> . . . he turned round and looked at Oliver, and
> called him by his name. He did not answer, and
> was to all appearances asleep.
>
> After satisfying himself upon this head, the Jew
> stepped gently to the door : which he fastened.
> He then drew forth : as it seemed to Oliver, from
> some trap in the floor : a small box, which he
> placed carefully on the table. His eyes glistened as
> he raised the lid, and looked in. Dragging an old
> chair to the table, he sat down ; and took from it a
> magnificent gold watch, sparkling with jewels.
>
> ' Aha ! ' said the Jew, shrugging up his shoulders,
> and distorting every feature with a hideous grin.
> ' Clever dogs ! Clever dogs ! Staunch to the last !
> Never told the old parson where they were. Never
> peached upon old Fagin ! And why should they ?
> It wouldn't have loosened the knot, or kept the drop
> up, a minute longer. No, no, no ! Fine fellows !
> Fine fellows ! '
>
> With these, and other muttered reflections of the

like nature, the Jew once more deposited the watch in its place of safety. At least half-a-dozen more were severally drawn forth from the same box, and surveyed with equal pleasure ; besides rings, brooches, bracelets, and other articles of jewellery, of such magnificent materials, and costly workmanship, that Oliver had no idea, even of their names. . . .

Obviously here Oliver's lack of taste and knowledge is manufactured into a claim upon our pity, whereas a French novelist—M. Pierre Loti, for example, and even, perhaps, M. Gide—would glory and the reader with him, rather, in young Oliver's estheticism, in his familiarity with lapis, sardonyx, ivory, jacinth, chrysoprasus and the rest of those precious materials so dear to the heart of the writer of ' Revelations ' : while the old ' fence ' himself would win a certain sympathy on account of his connoisseurship.

After the manner of Dickens, too, would Hogarth or the spendthrift Rowlandson have presented this gloating soliloquy of Fagin's, and with an identical gusto. Yet, on the other hand, and illogically enough, all of them were shocked by the lavish expenditure of the luxurious rich : they liked the poor to spend money they did not possess, more than they cared for the rich to waste that which they had. An English characteristic once more, I apprehend : as is Dickens' mortal distrust of lawyers and the law. Nevertheless, as well as sharing some of the national traits, he is expert at portraying others which he scorns: and where, psychologically speaking, this author was able to blaze a trail was in his revelation and treatment of that peculiarly Anglo-Saxon vice, hypocrisy; which, growing from a minute English-puritan root in the seventeenth-century, was in his day creeping like their own suffocating yellow fogs over life in the industrial cities of England and North America.

Unfortunately, though, just as the esthetic preferences of Samuel Butler are of less consequence to us, less new, stimulating and founded in self-discovered truth, than his esthetic feuds, so in Dickens' novels the personages of whom he manifests approval, indicating as virtuous and congenial friends for us, never succeed in capturing our imagination to the same extent as those whom he attacks, exposes and condemns. Yet they do not altogether fail, these virtuous and charming people: for we accept them as such, and are only forced to regret our own unhappy weakness for bad company, in that we prefer spending three hours in the thieves' kitchen to two minutes with dear old Mrs. Maylie: which is to say, they are apt to bore us but do not forfeit altogether our sympathy. Thus the pathetic touches about Little

44   Dorrit, or Dick in *Oliver Twist*, the fatiguing en-
comiums of Ruth Pinch, can induce, it is true, a
certain discomfort in the sensitive reader—a discomfort fully compensated in other respects by
the author's genius—yet they never wholly defeat
their own purpose by throwing him so violently,
and despite his inclinations, on the side of oppres-
sion and hypocrisy as to pray for the ultimate
success of Mr. Pecksniff or 'the man Monks':
whereas other writers, seemingly more impartial,
never wearing, as does this great novelist, a
heart carelessly pinned upon the sleeve, but rather
a half-heart, blazoned discreetly upon a partly
concealed and tear-stained handkerchief, uninten-
tionally inveigle us into a ferocious championship
of the licentious, malevolent and down-treading
against the persecuted and pure. Thus the quietly
argued, cautious pleading of Mr. Galsworthy, so
strictly unbiassed and wanting in any vulgar,
melodramatic appeal, often, so far from attaining
its object, persuades us to hope that the wealthy
and careless wastrel, who leaves silver boxes about
to tempt poor people, will prosper, and that the
respectable and 'really-awfully-nice' charwoman,
who has led so hard a life, will incur a severe and
quite unmerited punishment for a theft she has
never committed. Such *can* be the effects of a

sense of social justice in a writer ! But Dickens,
moreover, can win us, for a moment, to the very
side against which he has previously prejudiced us.
For example, let us take the account of Fagin in
the dock, waiting for the Judge to pronounce
sentence :

> He looked up to the gallery again. Some of the
> people were eating, and some fanning themselves
> with handkerchiefs ; for the crowded place was very
> hot. There was one young man sketching his face
> in a little notebook. He wondered whether it was
> like, and looked on when the artist broke his pencil-
> point, and made another with his knife, as any idle
> spectator might have done.
>
> In the same way, when he turned his eyes towards
> the Judge, his mind began to busy itself with the
> fashion of his dress, and what it cost, and how he
> put it on. There was an old fat gentleman on the
> bench, too, who had gone out, some half an hour
> before, and now came back. He wondered within
> himself whether this man had been to get his
> dinner, what he had had, and where he had had it ;
> and pursued this train of careless thought until
> some new object caught his eye and roused another.

Dickens, then, succeeds in convincing us, makes
us at any rate accept his point of view, by means
of his inflammatory and sustained arraignment of
iniquity, and also because he makes us understand
that it is not that he regards as a virtue poverty in

itself, but that he resents the rich behaving as if it were a crime. Each book of his discloses, crowded with figures, a wide panorama, in which there are always—so long as they are not misers—a few rich and virtuous people, and, inevitably, a great many poverty - stricken rogues. But, notwithstanding that he does not consider the rich naturally and wholly bad, it is undoubtedly a symptom of this author's dislike for any particular poor individual, in any one of his novels, should he display that character to us as eager to make money.

Again, in this we may detect a national trait : a love of fair play. The truth is, I apprehend, that Dickens' sense of social justice, above all his humanity, were too strong to allow him to attain to any ultimate perfection of art. But yet as a novelist he does not, as I once thought, stand entirely outside art : on the contrary, himself remains with one foot outside his novels, while by his art enticing you to enter and tarry a time. Once there, we soon know the people. They ring true to themselves, and we cannot step out of this life, cannot stop reading, until we are aware of what becomes of them. Thus Dickens resembles, it may be said, the God of the Old Testament, creating a world and its inhabitants whom he delights to punish and reward, rather than a

novelist reproducing the life round him. But his
greatness resides in this very fact. Triumphantly
he creates a world : and the creation is immense
and magnificent.

Indeed, if England were suddenly to be sub-
merged by the steely arrows of her rain beneath
her grey waves, and no vestige of her left save the
works of two authors, Shakespeare and Dickens,
yet our country would continue to possess a very
real existence in the minds of those who learnt to
read this dead language. Shakespeare would be
the guide to her permanent and rustic life, to that
ideal country of green, deep lanes and high green
banks, of wild flowers and oaks and elm-trees, of
scented limes and mysterious murmurings in the
woods at night, and of the old grey walls of hall
and cottage, buttressed against time and padded
with moss and lichen ; Dickens, to that dark
moment of sudden wealth, when, within a few
decades, her cities, losing all proportion to the land-
scape out of which they had grown, had swollen to
elephantine and meaningless dimensions, housing
as many people as in former ages had composed
entire nations, when the smoke of her chimneys
blackened the sky above her, and all her streams
were sullied with the filth of her factories.

Printed in Great Britain
by T. and A. Constable Ltd.
at the University Press
Edinburgh

'THE DOLPHIN BOOKS, well printed and charmingly covered, are signs of the times. Messrs. Chatto and Windus are demonstrating their faith in the new discovery that there are more lengths in literature than were dreamt of in the publishers' catalogues of the previous generation.'—*Time & Tide*.

The series is uniform Cr. 8vo in format, though the colour of the binding varies with each author. It includes and will include short original works of every kind —indeed its range is limited by size of volume alone. Each book costs but 2s. ; while there is often printed a small limited, and signed edition of books in the series, intended for the pleasure of the collector.

No. 1. VULGARITY IN LITERATURE

An essay by ALDOUS HUXLEY

'Mr. Huxley's essay is like all his work—keen criticism based on hard thinking.'—*Time & Tide*. *Vulgarity in Literature* contains a very remarkable analysis, (among much else of interest,) of the work of Edgar Allan Poe.

No. 2. ALCESTIS

Translated by RICHARD ALDINGTON

This is a lovely and scholarly rendering of the play of Euripides which is perhaps most significant of all his work to modern people.

No. 3. THE NEW PROVIDENCE
A story by R. H. MOTTRAM

An 'Easthampton' story written with all Mr. Mottram's skill and grace : full, too, of humour. 'Altogether delightful.'—*The Glasgow Herald*.

No. 4. THOMAS STEARNS ELIOT
An essay by THOMAS MCGREEVY

'Admirable . . . a very lucid performance—criticism of the right (and rare) kind, in short, constructive.'—*Norman Douglas*.

'He marks every sentence with the imprint of his own personality, and a very delightful personality it is.'—Rebecca West in *The Daily Telegraph*.

No. 5. THE ONLY PENITENT
A story by T. F. POWYS

'Mr. Powys is master of writing with a personal rhythm perfectly according with the idea to be expressed—a Gothic conception and style fashioned with the rarest artifice.'—*The Morning Post*.

No. 6. OPUS 7
A poem by SYLVIA TOWNSEND WARNER

'People call it her best work. This is high praise, but we think opinion will justify it.'—*The Observer*.

'A lovely work, coloured and shapely, and clear as a spring evening.'—*Country Life*.

No. 7. PROUST
An essay by SAMUEL BECKETT

Proust is a master who deserves criticism as intricate and careful as his own work. Mr. Beckett here proves himself a real interpreter.

'An excellent work, for Mr. Beckett is a very brilliant young man.'—*The Daily Telegraph*.

No. 8. LONDON STREET GAMES

An essay by NORMAN DOUGLAS

'Every one ought to buy this book.'—*The Observer*.

There is no book on London games approaching this in keenness of observation and carefulness of record. Mr. Douglas has seen games played in the London slums which are now only memories, and his book is not only a literary treasure, (something really new in style,) but one for which future historians and antiquarians will bless him.

No. 9. THE FAR-OFF HILLS

A comedy by LENNOX ROBINSON

When this play first appeared in the West End, *The Bystander* averred that 'Mr. Robinson has brought laughter to London.' Here it is offered to readers, who will surely enjoy it in their studies as much as it is always enjoyed from the stalls, circles, and galleries of theatres.

No. 10. RICHARD ALDINGTON :
AN ENGLISHMAN

An essay by THOMAS McGREEVY

This essay, wise, temperate, and sympathetic, will place in a proper perspective the works of an author whose vitality and creative force will be a powerful influence on our future literature. Particularly interesting is Mr. McGreevy's examination of *Death of a Hero* and *The Colonel's Daughter*, Mr. Aldington's justly celebrated novels. It is an essay which is critical in the best sense. It is as lucid and charming as *Thomas Stearns Eliot*, by the same author.

No. 11. WRITERS AT WORK

By LOUISE MORGAN

Really intimate portraits of such diverse modern writers as W. B. Yeats, Somerset Maugham, Richard Aldington, Sinclair Lewis, A. E. Coppard, Sylvia Townsend Warner, Edgar Wallace, and Wyndham Lewis.

No. 12. NORMAN DOUGLAS

An essay by H. M. Tomlinson

An appreciation of the author of *South Wind* and other books of paramount importance in modern letters. Mr. Tomlinson examines Mr. Douglas's influence critically in an essay at once penetrating and understanding. It is a work which has long been needed.

No. 13. STEPPING HEAVENWARD

A satire by Richard Aldington

Here is related the life of the Blessed Jeremy Cibber, how he was born and raised in the U.S.A., how he came to Europe, conquered England, and was at length beatified, shortly after death, to the acclamations of the world. Vigorous satire is an uncommon fruit nowadays ; *Stepping Heavenward* is a ripe branch.

No. 14. WYNDHAM LEWIS

An essay by Roy Campbell

In this essay—an estimation by one modern of another—Mr. Campbell endeavours to assess at their true value the baffling talents, creative and critical, which have made Mr. Lewis the most prominent controversialist of our time and one of its most original writers and artists.

No. 15. THE PEOPLE'S OPERA

An essay by George Antheil

A summary of the whole modern opera movement in France, Italy, and more particularly in Germany, written with expert knowledge.

¶ *All the above titles are either ready or will be issued forthwith. Other volumes are in active preparation by Messrs. Chatto and Windus,* 97 & 99 *St. Martin's Lane, London, W.C.* 2.